My Daily Diet: Vegetables

On My Plate

On My Plate

My Daily Diet: Vegetables

Celicia Scott

Mason Crest

Mason Crest
450 Parkway Drive, Suite D
Broomall, PA 19008
www.masoncrest.com

Printed and bound in the United States of America.

9 8 7 6 5 4 3 2

Series ISBN: 978-1-4222-3094-7
ISBN: 978-1-4222-3100-5
ebook ISBN: 978-1-4222-8791-0

Library of Congress Cataloging-in-Publication Data

Scott, Celicia, 1957- author.
  My daily diet : vegetables / Celicia Scott.
      pages cm. — (On my plate)
  Audience: 9+
  Audience: Grade 4 to 6.
  Includes bibliographical references and index.
  ISBN 978-1-4222-3100-5 (hardback) — ISBN 978-1-4222-3094-7 (series) — ISBN 978-1-4222-8791-0 (ebook) 1. Vegetables in human nutrition—Juvenile literature. 2. Vegetables—Juvenile literature. I. Title.
  QP144.V44S36 2015
  613.2—dc23
                                    2014010568

Contents

KEY ICONS TO LOOK FOR:

 Text-Dependent Questions: These questions send the reader back to the text for more careful attention to the evidence presented there.

 Words to Understand: These words with their easy-to-understand definitions will increase the reader's understanding of the text, while building vocabulary skills.

 Series Glossary of Key Terms: This back-of-the book glossary contains terminology used throughout this series. Words found here increase the reader's ability to read and comprehend higher-level books and articles in this field.

 Research Projects: Readers are pointed toward areas of further inquiry connected to each chapter. Suggestions are provided for projects that encourage deeper research and analysis.

 Sidebars: This boxed material within the main text allows readers to build knowledge, gain insights, explore possibilities, and broaden their perspectives by weaving together additional information to provide realistic and holistic perspectives.

Introduction

Most of us would agree that building healthy bodies and minds is a critical component of future success in school, work, and life. Providing our bodies with adequate and healthy nutrition in childhood sets the stage for both optimal learning and healthy habits in adulthood. Research suggests that the epidemic of overweight and obesity in young children leads to a large medical and financial burden, both for individuals and society. Children who are overweight and obese are more likely to become overweight or obese adults, and they are also at increased risk for a range of diseases.

Developing healthy eating and fitness habits in childhood is one of the most important gifts we can all provide to children in our homes and workplaces—but as any parent can attest, this is not always an easy task! Children are surrounded with both healthy and unhealthy eating options in their homes, schools, and in every restaurant or store they visit. Glossy marketing of food and meals is ubiquitous in media of all types, impacting both children's and adults' eating choices. As a result of the multiple influences on eating choices, from infancy through adulthood, we all benefit from additional support in making healthy choices.

Just as eating and fitness can become habits in adulthood, personal decision-making in childhood is critical to developing healthy habits. Providing healthy options and examples are a starting point, which can support children's healthy habits, but children also benefit from understanding the rationale for eating reasonable portions of healthy foods. Parents, teachers, and others often communicate messages through their words and actions—but books can provide more detailed information and pictures.

Building on this need for developing informed consumers, the ON MY PLATE series provides elementary school children with an informative yet fun introduction to their eating options. Beginning with an introduction to the five food groups, children can learn about what they ideally will have on their own plate and in their mouths. Tips are provided for choosing healthy snacks. And children will understand the importance of eating a range of foods. These books empower our children to make healthy decisions for themselves.

An additional benefit of this series may be the trickle-up effect for parents. Even if we all *know* the importance of making healthy choices for meals and snacks, there's nothing like a child *reminding us* why this is important. When our children start citing the long-term consequences of our dietary choices, we tend to listen!

Here's to developing healthy eating habits today!

Lisa Albers Prock, MD, MPH
Developmental Behavioral Pediatrician, Boston Children's Hospital
Assistant Professor, Harvard Medical School

WORDS TO UNDERSTAND

greenhouses: Buildings made of glass or transparent plastic, which let light in but keep heat from leaving.

pesticides: Poisonous chemicals used to kill the animals that eat crops.

seedlings: Baby plants that have just sprouted from their seeds.

till: To prepare land to grow crops on it.

Chapter 1

Where Do Vegetables Come From?

Everything you eat comes from somewhere. Food doesn't just magically appear on grocery store shelves or on your table at home. In fact, many people are involved in getting food on your plate.

To really understand where food comes from, you'll have to follow it all the way back to its starting point. Take vegetables, for example. You can follow vegetables from the farm to your plate, with several stops along the way.

PLANTS AND DIRT

All vegetables are plants. They grow in the ground and need water and sunlight to grow.

Vegetables are actually different parts of the plant. Think about all the parts a plant has—roots, stems, leaves, flowers, and fruits. We eat all those parts in the form of different vegetables!

Different parts of a plant have different nutrients and chemicals in them. That's why we can eat the roots of some plants, but not the leaves—or the leaves of some plants, but not the stems!

MAKE CONNECTIONS

Not all vegetables go through the same process. Some are grown on smaller farms and sold to people who live nearby. Farmers take their vegetables to farmers' markets or sell them right on the farm. There aren't any trucks, planes, warehouses, factories, or grocery stores involved. People buy locally grown vegetables, because they are often fresher and tastier. People also like to meet and talk to the farmers. And these vegetables haven't had to travel halfway across the world on vehicles that use a lot of gas. Transportation is a big part of climate change, so using less transportation is one way to fight climate change. It's also a way to support small, local, and often family farms.

Many vegetables are roots. Carrots, potatoes, onions, and beets are all roots, because they grow underground.

A few vegetables are stems, or at least have stems we eat. Celery is a stem, and so is asparagus. Spinach and lettuce have stems, too, which we eat along with the rest of the vegetable.

Speaking of spinach and lettuce, they are all leaves. Other leafy vegetables include chard, collard greens, and kale.

We also eat one or two vegetables that are actually flowers. Broccoli and cauliflower are both flower buds that haven't opened yet!

Fruit vegetables are probably the trickiest plant part to understand. In terms of their biology, fruits are really anything with seeds in them. The fruits you're used to—like oranges, apples, and strawberries—all have seeds. They're all sweet, and you generally don't have to cook them before eating. When we talk about plant parts and biology, we have a bigger definition of fruit in mind. Any vegetables with seeds in them are also considered fruits. You still wouldn't call them fruits if you're talking about cooking or eating. But if you're talking about plant parts and biology, you would. Lots of vegetables are biologically fruits, because they have seeds in them. Cucumbers, peppers, tomatoes, eggplants, and squash are all biologically fruits.

No matter if they're stems, leaves, roots, or fruits, most vegetables are grown on farms. The vegetables you and your family buy in the store came from farms around the world.

Many vegetable farms are huge. Thousands of peppers or heads of lettuce are harvested at once. There are hundreds and hundreds of rows of vegetables.

Harvesting is the last step in the growing process. Many steps have to happen on the farm before the vegetables can be picked and make their way to your plate. First, seeds are planted in the ground. Sometimes seeds are started in **greenhouses**. Once they grow into tiny **seedlings**, they are planted in the ground. Then the seeds or seedlings are watered. When they get bigger, some farmers will spray them with pesticides to keep away bugs that will eat the plants. Eventually, the plants get big enough to harvest.

Some vegetables take just a few weeks to grow. Lettuce, for example, grows pretty fast.

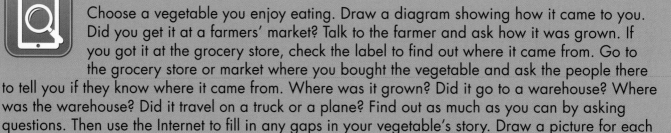

RESEARCH PROJECT

Choose a vegetable you enjoy eating. Draw a diagram showing how it came to you. Did you get it at a farmers' market? Talk to the farmer and ask how it was grown. If you got it at the grocery store, check the label to find out where it came from. Go to the grocery store or market where you bought the vegetable and ask the people there to tell you if they know where it came from. Where was it grown? Did it go to a warehouse? Where was the warehouse? Did it travel on a truck or a plane? Find out as much as you can by asking questions. Then use the Internet to fill in any gaps in your vegetable's story. Draw a picture for each step of the story. Label each step's picture and then make an arrow that leads to the next step.

Tomatoes, on the other hand, take a long time to grow. The plant has to get big and strong first. Then it forms blossoms, followed by tomato fruits with seeds inside. The small, green fruits grow larger, and their color usually changes from green to red. There are also varieties that stay green or turn yellow or red when ripe. It takes a few months for tomatoes to be ready to eat. But they are well worth the wait!

Once the vegetables are harvested, they're ready for the next step on their way to your plate.

WAREHOUSES AND FACTORIES

Vegetables don't usually go straight from the farm to the grocery store. They have to go somewhere else first.

Some vegetables go to warehouses owned by the stores. Cucumbers that are going to be sold whole and fresh, for example, would go to a warehouse. They are picked up by a truck from the farm where they were harvested. Then they are brought to the warehouse, where they are kept until they can be sent on to the store.

Lots of the canned and bagged foods in grocery stores have vegetables in them. Vegetable foods that aren't whole and fresh are called processed foods. Tomato sauce is a good example. Tomato sauce has tomatoes and maybe onions, garlic, and mushrooms. Tomato sauce is a processed food, because you're not buying whole tomatoes, onions, garlic, and mushrooms and making it yourself. Factories make processed foods out of vegetables.

Some are simple processed foods, where not much is done to the vegetables. Some vegetables are canned. One factory might cut up carrots and put them in cans. Another might slice up cucumbers and make them into pickles. A third might cut corn off the cob and freeze it in bags.

Other factories make more complicated processed foods. Vegetable soup, vegetable chips, and pickles are all examples of processed vegetable foods made by factories.

TEXT-DEPENDENT QUESTIONS

1. The chapter says there are multiple steps in getting vegetables to your plate. What is the first step?
2. What are the parts of a plant from which we can get vegetables?
3. Explain why vegetables like tomatoes and cucumbers are also fruits.
4. Name some of the people involved in getting vegetables to your table, and what they do.
5. What are local vegetables?

STORES

After the vegetables have made it to the warehouses and factories, they have one last big journey to make. They need to get to the stores where customers like you buy them.

Vegetables travel by truck, train, plane, and ship. Fresh vegetables have to get to stores pretty quickly, before they start to spoil. Processed vegetable foods don't have to travel so quickly. A jar of tomato sauce isn't going to go bad in just a few days.

Some vegetables travel all the way across the country or halfway around the world to get to a grocery store. Your lettuce might have come from California or Brazil. If you live in Hawaii or Toronto, it had to travel a long way to get to you.

Once the vegetables have made it to the grocery store, they go on the shelves. Customers like you come along and pick the ones they want. Then it's through the checkout and into kitchens and stomachs.

PEOPLE

Many people are involved in getting vegetables from the farm to the table. First are the farmers and farmworkers who grow the vegetables. On big farms, farmers are more like businesspeople. They decide what to grow, how much to grow, and where to sell it. Farmworkers do the hard work of planting and harvesting the vegetables.

On smaller farms, farmers do more of the work in the fields. They *till* the soil, plant, water, protect the crops, and pick them.

After the farm, someone has to drive the vegetables to a warehouse or factory. People at the warehouse or factory unload the vegetables and deliver them where they need to go. At warehouses, more people load the vegetables onto other trucks to travel to stores. At factories, people process the vegetables and make them into other foods.

At the grocery store, more people unload the vegetables and put them on shelves. Workers at the cash register scan the vegetables and put them into bags. And finally, someone cooks the vegetables before they're eaten!

WORDS TO UNDERSTAND

unsaturated fat: A type of fat that is considered to be healthier for humans, often from plant sources.

digestive system: The parts of your body that work together to break down food and absorb nutrients.

minerals: A substance that can often be found naturally in metals or rocks. We need very small amounts of certain minerals to be healthy.

kale: A kind of cabbage with large, edible leaves.

Chapter 2

Why Do I Need to Eat Vegetables Every Day?

You may be tired of people telling you to eat vegetables all the time. Maybe you'd rather eat other things—like ice cream and chips. But do a little investigating, and you'll see why vegetables are so good for you. Don't take other people's word for it. Find out for yourself.

NUTRIENTS

Vegetables are so healthy because of nutrients. Nutrients are the building blocks of food. These very tiny particles make up all foods. Some of the more commonly known nutrients are calcium, vitamin C, and protein.

Nutrients are one of the reasons people need to eat food. Every nutrient does something

MAKE CONNECTIONS

Sugar is a type of carbohydrate. And we need carbohydrates to stay healthy. So can you just eat as much sugar as you want? Definitely not. In small amounts, sugar provides energy to keep you going through your day. Fruits are a great example of a sugar that will give you a healthy amount of energy. However, lots of people eat too much sugar. Eating too much of a nutrient can be just as harmful as not eating enough. Eating too much sugar at once, like eating a candy bar or drinking a soda, will give you too much all at once. You'll get a burst of energy followed by a crash and maybe a headache or stomachache. Over time, eating too much sugar leads to health problems, like obesity and diabetes.

Not every food has every nutrient that you need, so you should eat a lot of different kinds of food. For example, most vegetables don't have the fat that your body needs—or the carbohydrates to give you energy.

MAKE CONNECTIONS

Nutritionists like to use the word "antioxidants" when they're describing healthy food. Every day, your body creates tiny substances called free radicals. Breathing, digesting, and activities like smoking all create free radicals. Those free radicals can attack cells and may, over time, make people sick. Luckily, substances in food called antioxidants protect cells from free radicals. Vegetables have a lot of antioxidants. In fact, antioxidant is just a fancy name for some of the nutrients you already know—like vitamins A, C, and E. Other antioxidants include selenium, lycopene, and lutein. In general, the darker colored the vegetable, the more antioxidants it has.

different for the body. Working together, nutrients keep your body strong, healthy, and working right.

There are dozens of nutrients. We need to eat large amounts of some nutrients. Those nutrients are called macronutrients.

One macronutrient is protein. Protein provides energy and makes muscles strong. Another macronutrient is fat. You may think fat is unhealthy, but people need to eat some fat to survive. Certain kinds of fats, like **unsaturated fat**, are really important for health. Finally, carbohydrates are the third kind of macronutrient. Carbohydrates include sugar, starch, and fiber. Sugar and starch provide energy. Fiber keeps your **digestive system** moving and healthy.

Other nutrients are called micronutrients. We only need to eat small amounts of them. But without them, people get sick, and their bodies don't work right.

Vitamins and **minerals** are both micronutrients. Vitamins are nutrients that come from living things, like plants and animals. A plant makes some vitamins while it's growing. Then we eat that plant to get the vitamins. Vitamins have letter names, so there are vitamins A, B, C, D, E, and K.

Minerals are the other type of micronutrient. Plants and animals do not make minerals. They mostly come from the ground. A plant might suck up magnesium from the soil. When we eat the plant, our body takes in some of that magnesium. Common minerals include iron, calcium, potassium, and manganese.

VEGETABLE NUTRIENTS

Vegetables have many nutrients. They don't have every nutrient there is in the world, but they have a lot of them!

Many vegetables are high in vitamin A. Vitamin A helps you see. It keeps your skin and eyes healthy. It also helps prevent you from getting sick by boosting your immune system. Sweet potatoes, carrots, **kale**, and spinach are good sources of vitamin A.

Another vitamin, vitamin C is commonly found in vegetables. Vitamin C also keeps you from getting sick by protecting against infections. It helps the body heal if it's sick or injured. Vitamin C also keeps gums and teeth healthy.

Different nutrients often interact with each other, too. Vitamin C helps the body use iron and calcium, other nutrients. Cauliflower, broccoli, potatoes, and tomatoes have high levels of vitamin C.

Potassium is another nutrient found in some vegetables. Potassium helps your muscles and nerves work right. It also keeps blood pressure healthy. High blood pressure can lead to all sorts of health problems, like heart attacks and strokes. Broccoli, carrots, potatoes, and artichokes all have high levels of potassium.

A few vegetables are high in iron. Blood cells use iron to carry oxygen all over the body. Without that oxygen, you would feel really tired all the time. Iron keeps energy levels high by keeping oxygen levels in the blood up. Soybeans, spinach, chard, and beets are all good sources of iron.

Almost all vegetables have some fiber. Fiber is a different kind of nutrient, because we don't actually digest it. Fiber goes through the digestive system without being absorbed into the body. That doesn't mean it's not important, though! Fiber keeps the digestive system moving. Brussels sprouts, corn, broccoli, and carrots have a lot of fiber.

EATING BY COLOR

You don't need to memorize which vegetables have which nutrients. You can use colors to remember how a vegetable will keep you healthy. The color guide is also useful for fruits.

TEXT-DEPENDENT QUESTIONS

1. The chapter says vegetables are healthy for you. How are they healthy?
2. The chapter tells us vegetables do not make minerals. So how do we get minerals by eating vegetables?
3. What are macronutrients, and how are they important to your health? What vegetables contain macronutrients?
4. What are micronutrients, and how are they important to your health? What vegetables contain macronutrients?
5. What vegetables are believed to help prevent cancer?

Many red vegetables have lots of vitamin C along with other nutrients. Red vegetables protect your heart and blood vessels. They might even help prevent certain kinds of cancer. Tomatoes, beets, red peppers, and radishes have lots of vitamin C.

Orange and yellow vegetables tend to have lots of vitamin A. Many people have heard that carrots help you see better. That's partly true! Carrots and other orange and yellow vegetables, like sweet potatoes and yellow peppers, have vitamin A, which does keep eyes and vision healthy. Many orange and yellow vegetables also have vitamin C.

Green vegetables often have a lot of iron in them. Dark, leafy greens like collards, kale, and spinach have iron. Other green vegetables, like peas, also have iron. The same green vegetables have calcium too, which keeps your bones strong. Some green foods also have nutrients that protect eyesight.

Scientists think some blue and purple vegetables help fight cancer. These vegetables also keep the brain healthy and may improve memory. Eggplants, purple potatoes, and purple peppers are examples.

White and brown vegetables offer protection against some kinds of cancer, too. They protect against heart disease and keep the digestive system healthy. White and brown vegetables include garlic, onions, potatoes, and cauliflower.

If you eat all the colors, you'll be getting the full benefits of vegetables. By eating every color, you get a wide range of all the nutrients vegetables have. You'll be healthier, and your plate will be a lot more colorful!

WORDS TO UNDERSTAND

legumes: A food made from the seed of a plant, such as beans.

vegetarian: A person who doesn't eat meat. There are a few kinds of vegetarian, including lacto-ovo vegetarians, who eat eggs and milk, and vegans, who don't eat any food products from animals.

Chapter 3

So Why Can't I Just Eat Vegetables Every Day?

If vegetables are so healthy, and if you care about your health, you might be tempted to just eat vegetables every day. That wouldn't be a very good idea, though. Limiting yourself to just vegetables leaves out a lot of other healthy foods!

A BALANCED DIET

To be truly healthy, you need to think about food groups. We tend to think about food in five different groups. Eating healthy means eating from all five food groups.

Vegetables are one food group. Fruits are another. Sometimes fruits are lumped together with vegetables. They are plants, too. Fruits contain similar nutrients but tend to be sweeter. People don't cook fruits as often as they cook vegetables. They usually eat them raw.

Diet might refer to a special eating plan—or it might refer to all the foods you eat. Eating nothing but vegetables all the time wouldn't be a very healthy diet!

MAKE CONNECTIONS

Not all grains are equal. Some grains we eat are whole grains. When a grain is picked, it has three parts to it. Each part has nutrients. When the grain is sent to a factory, the factory often takes out two of those parts. The nutrients in those parts disappear. Grains with only one part left are called refined grains. They tend to last a little longer on shelves. Refined grains are often lighter in color, like white rice and white bread (made from refined wheat). Other grains still have all their parts when they get to the grocery store, so they still have all their nutrients. They're called whole grains and tend to be browner than refined grains. Brown rice and whole-wheat bread (made from whole wheat) are whole grains and are healthier. But be sure to read labels. Not all brown breads are made from whole grains. Others have only small amounts of whole grains. Choose to eat whole grains whenever you can!

Grains are another food group. Grains are the seeds of grass plants. They come from the ground, too. Rice is a grain. So are wheat, oats, barley, and corn.

Protein foods are a fourth food group. Meat is a protein food. So are beans, *legumes*, nuts, and eggs. If a food has a lot of protein in it, it's in this group.

The last food group is dairy. All dairy foods come from animal milk. Cheese, yogurt, cream, and, of course, milk are all dairy foods.

Each of these food groups have different nutrients. Fruits and vegetables have many vitamins and minerals, like vitamin C and potassium. Grains have iron, a little protein, and more vitamins and minerals. Protein foods have, obviously, a lot of protein. Dairy has calcium, among other nutrients.

When you eat food from every food group, you're getting some of all the nutrients. That's called a balanced diet.

When people talk about diets, they can mean different things. Sometimes people talk about going on a diet, which means they are only eating certain things or eating less food to lose weight.

But diet can also just mean the kinds and amounts of food you eat on average every day. Your diet might be made up of mostly junk food, which would be an unhealthy diet. Or you might not eat meat and have a *vegetarian* diet. If you have a balanced diet, you eat food from every food group every day.

SOME EXAMPLES

Let's say you really love vegetables. You want to eat vegetables all day, every day, and nothing else. Even further, you really just like tomatoes. You can't get enough of them, so you eat them for breakfast, lunch, and dinner.

RESEARCH PROJECT

Make a list of your favorite foods from each of the 5 food groups. Keep track of how often you eat them during a week. Were they cooked or raw? Are they prepared the same way each time? Did you have them at home, school, or a restaurant?

People often think of fat as a bad thing, but our bodies need some fat to work right. Some of the best foods to get our fat from are avocados, nuts, and certain kinds of fish.

TEXT-DEPENDENT QUESTIONS

1. What is a balanced diet, and why is it important?
2. What are the 5 food groups?
3. What can the word "diet" refer to?
4. The chapter says you can't eat just one food a day. Why not?
5. What are the benefits of eating whole grains?

Tomatoes are pretty healthy on their own. They have vitamins A, C, and K. They are high in potassium and have a lot of fiber. These are nutrients you need every day, so tomatoes are a healthy choice.

However, tomatoes don't have a lot of other nutrients you need. They don't have much fat, protein, or iron. They're low in vitamins B and E. If all you ever ate were tomatoes, you wouldn't get any of these nutrients. Over time, you would get sick. Your body wouldn't work right anymore.

Clearly, you have to eat more than tomatoes every day. What about just vegetables? The same idea applies. All together, vegetables are high in important nutrients, like vitamins, iron, potassium, and fiber. But not many vegetables are good sources of fat, carbohydrates, and proteins. Again, that leaves out really important nutrients people need to eat every day.

A balanced diet includes all those nutrients, which means you'll need to eat from a variety of food groups. Of course, you should definitely include vegetables as part of that healthy diet! But eating protein foods adds protein to your diet. Eating grains adds more protein, vitamins, minerals, and carbohydrates. Dairy adds calcium and fat. When you eat a balanced diet, you're getting all the nutrients you need.

WORDS TO UNDERSTAND

U.S. Department of Agriculture (USDA): The part of the U.S. government that regulates farming and gives people advice on how to eat.

stir-fry: Pieces of various foods stirred in a frying pan and cooked quickly.

guideline: A piece of advice about the best way to do something.

allergic: When you body has a negative reaction to a substance that is normally harmless.

Chapter

4

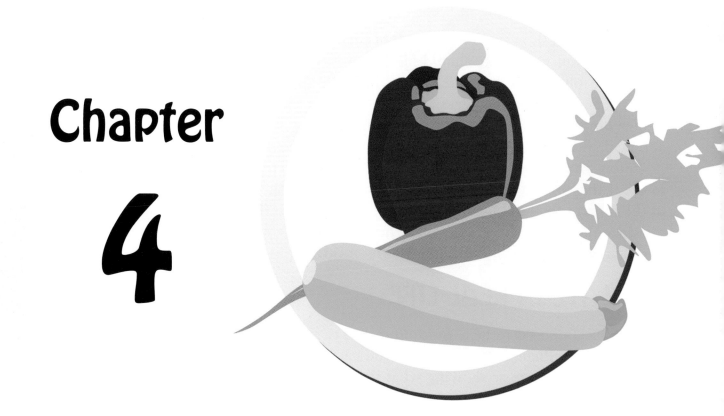

Putting Vegetables on My Plate Every Day

Eating enough vegetables every single day may sound hard. Luckily, there are tools to help you. One is MyPlate, created by the **U.S. Department of Agriculture**. MyPlate is designed to help people see just how much of each food group they should eat.

USING MYPLATE

MyPlate looks like it sounds—like a plate. It is divided into four sections of different colors, with a glass on the side.

Each section is one food group. On the left is a green section, which takes up a little more than one-quarter of the plate. The green section is labeled "Vegetables." Above that is a slightly smaller red section labeled "Fruits." The other half of the plate is divided in half again, into an orange "Grain" section and a purple "Protein" section. In the corner is a blue glass of milk labeled "Dairy."

Each section shows you how much of each food group you're supposed to eat at a meal. One-quarter of your plate should have grains. One-quarter should have proteins. A little more than one-quarter should have vegetables. And a little less than one-quarter should have fruits. Don't forget a glass of milk with your meal.

For dinner, you might be having a **stir-fry**. The stir-fry has broccoli, peppers, carrots, and beef, along with rice. You have some milk on the side and some fruit salad for dessert.

Before you mix all your food together, you could separate all those different food groups to see if they match MyPlate. The rice would go in the grain section. The beef would go in the protein section. The vegetables obviously go in the vegetable section. And the fruit salad would sit in the fruit section. The glass of milk would be to the side. If it looks like MyPlate, you're probably eating a healthy meal!

MYPLATE IN REAL LIFE

MyPlate is supposed to be a **guideline**. You're not always going to eat a meal that looks exactly like MyPlate. Not every meal you eat has every food group. And that's OK.

Think of MyPlate as showing what you should eat over a whole day. You should have food from all five food groups throughout the day, even if you don't eat one or two of those food groups during a meal.

For breakfast, you may eat toast with peanut butter and banana and drink glass of milk. You ate some grains (the toast), fruit (the banana), a little protein (the peanut butter), and dairy (the milk). You didn't eat any vegetables, though.

You'll have to make sure to eat vegetables for lunch, since you didn't have any for breakfast. Try a salad with lots of veggies. Have some crackers and cheese for extra grains and dairy. Then you can have some of that stir-fry for dinner, along with fruit salad and milk. If you look back over your whole day, you'll see you ate every food group.

MyPlate also shows you the balance of food groups you should eat during the day. The plate and cup show that you need about equal amounts of each food group, with a little more vegetables.

Eating one carrot over a whole day and mostly food from the other groups isn't very balanced. Eating every food group except protein for days at a time isn't very healthy or balanced, either. Pay attention to how much of each food group you eat, not just the food groups themselves.

Sometimes people don't eat all five food groups for very specific reasons. Some people are **allergic** to some foods or can't digest them very well. For example, some people can't digest dairy very well. They feel sick if they drink milk or eat cheese.

Still other people choose not to eat certain food groups or foods from certain food groups for personal reasons. Someone might decide to be vegetarian and not eat meat, because he thinks killing and eating animals is wrong. Or someone who is Muslim or Jewish may choose not to eat pork for religious reasons.

These people can still be healthy and have balanced diets. They just have to pay a little more attention to what they eat. People who can't eat dairy are losing out on the calcium,

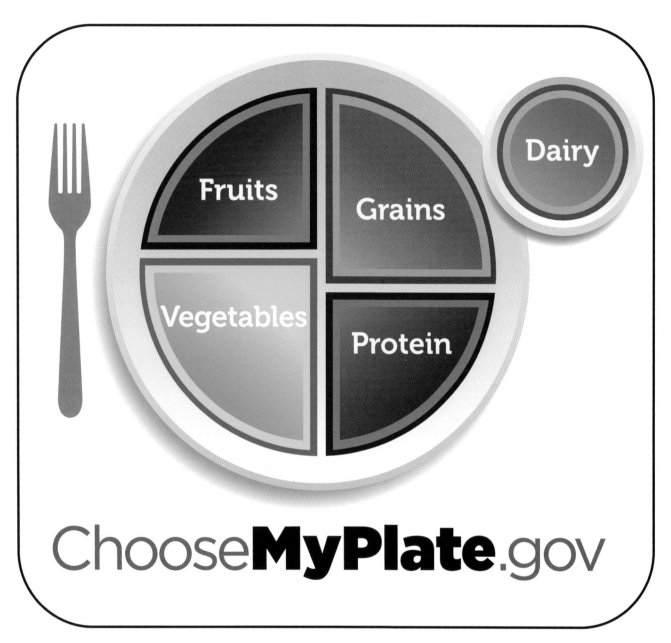

The USDA's MyPlate helps you get an idea of how much of each food group you should be eating—whether you eat a lot or a little bit of food every day.

protein, fats, and vitamins that dairy has. Luckily, other foods have all these nutrients. They need to know what those foods are and eat them often. Instead of dairy, they can eat more dark green vegetables, like kale, which have calcium.

A vegetarian may not get enough protein, because she isn't eating meat. She can eat other foods from the protein group, like beans and nuts. She just has to make sure to eat enough of these foods to make up for not eating meat.

RESEARCH PROJECT

Help your parents plan meals for the week that fall within MyPlate guidelines. Ask your family what kind of foods they like. Include those to make the meal plan more attractive. Help your parents shop for groceries to make the items on the menu. Help cook and serve the meals when possible. When the week is over, write about the experience. What did you learn? Were there surprises? How well did you and your family stick to MyPlate guidelines?

MEASURING IT OUT

The MyPlate website also gives you some advice on how many vegetables to eat every day. The amount you need changes with age. Here are the MyPlate recommendations for how many vegetables to eat over a whole day:

- toddlers age 2 to 3: one cup
- children age 4 to 8: one and a half cups
- girls age 9 to 13: two cups
- boys age 9 to 13: two and a half cups
- girls age 14 to 18: two and a half cups
- boys age 14 to 18: three cups
- women age 19 to 50: two and a half cups
- men age 19 to 50: three cups
- women over 50: two cups
- men over 50: two and a half cups

How many vegetables you need depends on your age and sex. Boys and men generally need more vegetables (and more food in general) than girls and women. You also need more vegetables as you get older, at least until you're 50.

MAKE CONNECTIONS

You'll notice that junk food isn't anywhere on MyPlate. There's no section labeled "Junk Food." Junk food is food that doesn't have a lot of healthy nutrients and has too much of certain nutrients, like lots of salt, sugar, and fat. You need a little bit of each of those nutrients but not a lot. Junk food, like chips, candy, and cookies, have way too much of them. Junk food is a special-occasion food, not food to eat every day. Over time, eating too much junk food can lead to unhealthy weight gain, diabetes, and other health problems.

TEXT-DEPENDENT QUESTIONS

1. What is MyPlate?
2. According to MyPlate, how much of your plate should be taken up by proteins?
3. What determines how many vegetables you should eat every day?
4. How can vegetarians get the nutrients they may be missing by not eating meat?
5. What is the problem with junk food?

How many vegetables you need also depends on how active you are. If you're especially active, or if you do sports, you need more vegetables than this chart says. In fact, you need more food in general. Food is fuel for bodies, so if you use your body more, you need more fuel.

The chart on page 30 tells you how many vegetables you need in cups. That's not very helpful for everyday eating. You're probably not going to carry around a measuring cup and see how much you're eating!

You can think about how the vegetables you normally eat compare to a cup. If your hands are small, filling your cupped hands with cut-up raw or cooked vegetables might be about a cup. Two cups of leafy greens count as one cup of vegetables. And two cups of leafy greens is about as big as a medium-sized salad. A glass of vegetable juice also counts as a cup of vegetables.

Here are some estimates of how vegetables compare to one cup:

1 cup equals:
- 2 carrots, whole or cut up
- 1 large tomato, whole or cut up
- a mound of mashed potatoes
- 8 ounces of vegetable juice
- 1 ear of corn
- 6 broccoli florets
- 1 large pepper, whole or cut up

But don't stop there. The general rule is the more vegetables the better!

WORDS TO UNDERSTAND

hummus: A dip made of mashed chick peas and various seasonings.
kabobs: Small pieces of food grilled on a skewer.

Chapter 5

Fast Foods, Snacks, and Vegetables

You can eat vegetables at every single meal. And you can choose to eat vegetables at home, school, and in restaurants.

The most challenging place to eat vegetables is often fast-food restaurants. People think of hamburgers and french fries when they think of fast food, not vegetables. But with a little menu hunting, you can even find some vegetables to make your fast-food meal a little healthier.

And don't forget snacks! You can even eat vegetables between meals for delicious, healthy snacks.

FAST FOOD

You won't get all the vegetables you need at a fast-food restaurant, but you can search for the vegetables that are there.

MAKE CONNECTIONS

Eat vegetables at breakfast. Cook some scrambled eggs, and add in your vegetables of choice, like spinach and peppers. Or make an omelet and layer in veggies like spinach, mushrooms, tomatoes, and onions. Potatoes are also a great choice for breakfast. Roast some potatoes or sweet potatoes and make home fries. Some people even blend kale into their smoothies, which adds a lot of nutrients and not too much vegetable taste to your breakfast. For other vegetable breakfast drinks, try carrot juice.

Having a few vegetables with every meal is a great way to make sure you get enough in your diet.

MAKE CONNECTIONS

Try this recipe for homemade salsa:

Ingredients: 3 large tomatoes, 2 cloves garlic, ¼ cup onion, 1 hot pepper (optional), 2 tablespoons lime juice, 1 teaspoon salt, 1 tablespoon cilantro (optional)

Directions: Chop the tomatoes, garlic, onions, and hot pepper if using, and mix all together. Add in lime juice, salt, and cilantro if using. For a smoother salsa, put all ingredients to a blender or food processor and blend for a few seconds. Refrigerate for 2 hours for best results.

Sure, french fries are potatoes. So aren't they healthy? Not really. You need to think about how the vegetables are prepared, not just whether they are vegetables.

French fries are generally not very healthy for you. They are deep-fried in oil, so they're crunchy. Frying can add unhealthy fat. Plus, french fries have a lot of salt on them. Too much fat and salt aren't very healthy. It's OK to eat fast-food french fries once in a while, but limit how many times you eat them every week or month.

Most menus have some healthier vegetable options. Many places have salads with lettuce, tomatoes, cucumbers, and other vegetables. To make them as healthy as possible, choose the salads with grilled, not fried, meat. And keep the salad dressing light, like Italian, rather than heavy dressings, like ranch.

Some fast-food restaurants serve soup. Check out the soup selections for vegetables. You might find chili, vegetable soup, or broccoli cheddar soup.

A few fast-food restaurants have veggie burgers. They give you the same experience of eating a burger, without the meat and with more vegetables.

You also usually have the option of putting more vegetables on burgers and sandwiches. Ask for extra tomatoes and lettuce on your burger. Load up your sub with veggies. Make sure you add lots of vegetables to your burrito. Whenever you have the chance, go for more vegetables.

Don't forget the vegetable sides. Some places have sides like mashed potatoes, a baked potato, a small salad, or corn. Even if you get a regular hamburger or a taco or pizza without vegetables, you can add some vegetables on the side.

The next time you're at a fast-food restaurant, take a look at the menu. Look for the items with vegetables.

SNACKING ON VEGGIES

A great way to get more vegetables in your diet is through snacks. Snacks are like mini meals you eat between breakfast, lunch, and dinner.

Snacks can be a really healthy part of your day—if you choose to eat the right things. Eating candy or chips aren't healthy choices.

RESEARCH PROJECT

Most fast-food restaurants provide their customers with some nutritional information where they order. The next time you're at a restaurant, note what information is provided. You can often find more detailed information on the restaurant's website. Assume you're going to order your favorite meal, and write down its nutritional information. Then come up with a healthier alternative available at the same restaurant.

Keeping carrot sticks or other healthy snacks ready in your refrigerator will help you make healthy choices when you want to snack, instead of automatically eating junk food.

TEXT-DEPENDENT QUESTIONS

1. The chapter says you can have vegetables at every meal. How can you add vegetables to your breakfast?
2. What makes it so difficult to find healthy vegetable dishes at fast-food restaurants?
3. What makes fast-food french fries unhealthy?
4. Why can snacking on vegetables be a good food choice?
5. The chapter lists some vegetable snack ideas. What are some others?

Snacks are a good way to catch up on the food groups you haven't eaten enough of during the day. You may have eaten fruit, grains, protein, and dairy for breakfast and lunch, but you didn't eat any vegetables. You can sneak some in with a snack after lunch.

Vegetable snack ideas are almost endless. You might want to try:

- crackers with cream cheese and sliced cucumbers or radishes on top
- carrots, peppers, cucumbers, broccoli, tomatoes, or other vegetables dipped in **hummus** or yogurt dip
- ants on a log: celery spread with peanut butter and with raisins on top
- mini carrot muffins
- kale chips: bake kale with olive oil and salt for a few minutes; or skip the salt and have an even healthier snack.
- mini pizzas: whole-wheat English muffin with tomato sauce or pesto, a little cheese, and sliced tomatoes, broccoli, peppers, mushrooms, or other pizza veggies
- baked french fries made with potatoes or sweet potatoes
- vegetable **kabobs**: skewer small vegetables on a toothpick and serve with dip
- corn chips dipped in fresh salsa made with fresh tomatoes

Snacks are an important part of your diet. They're one piece of a bigger picture!

Healthy
Living

+

Diet
&
Exercise

Chapter 6

The Big Picture

Eating vegetables has a very important purpose—it keeps you healthy. Of course, they taste good, too, but that's just one reason to eat them.

Vegetables keep you healthy in all sorts of ways. They help you maintain a healthy weight. They keep your body healthy and strong right now. And they can keep you from getting seriously sick in the future.

HEALTHY WEIGHT

Weight isn't all about looking good; it's about being healthy. Everyone's body is different. Some people are healthier if they weigh less, and some are healthier if they weigh more.

Food is directly related to weight. Food contains calories. Calories measure how much energy a food has. A food with a lot of calories has a lot of energy. A food with few calories has much less energy.

Most people need to eat between 1,800 and 2,200 calories a day. Women, kids, and

Moving around and exercising burns calories—so normally, if you exercise a lot, you'll need to eat more food to fuel your body than someone who doesn't exercise much.

MAKE CONNECTIONS

Healthy diets are important, but so is exercise. Even if you eat a healthy diet, if you never moved, you would probably not be very healthy. Get as much exercise as you can. Play games with friends, run or jog, take walks or hikes, join a sports team. Whatever you do, don't just sit in front of the TV or computer for hours every day. You're missing out on health and fun! Exercise keeps your heart, muscles, bones, and more healthy. And it helps keeps you at a healthy weight.

people who are less active need fewer calories. Men and people who are more active need more calories.

When you eat fewer calories than you need every day, you lose weight. When you eat more calories than you need, you gain weight.

Many foods with the highest number of calories are junk foods. They have lots of sugar, fat, and salt in them, which helps increase the number of calories. For example, one fast-food meal may have more than 1,000 calories! That's over half the calories you need in an entire day. Plus, that meal comes along with unhealthy amounts of nutrients.

Vegetables, on the other hand, are low in calories. You can eat lots of them and not worry about how many calories you're eating. Plus, those vegetables have a lot of good nutrients. The healthiest foods are low in calories and high in good nutrients, like vitamins and minerals.

Eating vegetables helps you keep your weight healthy. Remember, a healthy weight is a sign that you have enough energy to get through your day, you're growing the way you should, and your body is working correctly. A healthy weight does not mean you're really skinny. For some people, skinny is healthy. For others, it's very unhealthy. It all depends on your body!

HEALTHY TODAY

Eating vegetables keeps you healthy right now. All those nutrients in vegetables keep your body running strong. Vitamin A protects your eyes. Calcium builds bones. Iron keeps your energy up. Fiber keeps your digestive system working.

The great thing is that you can actually feel when you're healthy! Pay more attention to how you feel after you eat certain foods. When you eat junk food, you might feel like you don't have much energy. You may feel like taking a nap. You might get a headache or a stomachache. You're not at your best.

But if you eat vegetables, you might feel a lot better. Your stomach doesn't hurt. You have a lot of energy. Once you realize you actually feel better when you eat healthy foods, it's a lot easier to choose to eat them. Why would you choose junk foods all the time when they make you feel bad?

When people eat too many unhealthy fats and sugars, their bodies can lose the ability to produce insulin correctly. The result is type 2 diabetes. When this happens, people must keep track of their blood sugar, often with blood tests like this one—and they must be especially careful about what they eat.

Vegetables and other healthy foods also keep you from getting sick. Nutrients like vitamin C boost your immune system, which fights sickness. A healthy immune system, and a healthy body in general, is better able to fight off sickness. More vegetables may mean getting fewer colds and avoiding more serious illnesses, like the *flu*.

Vegetables aren't magic protection, though. You'll still probably get sick from time to time even if you eat really healthfully. But you may notice you're getting sick less often, and when you do, it doesn't last as long. That leaves more time to do the things you love!

FUTURE HEALTH

Of course, vegetables also protect your future health. The more vegetables and healthy foods you eat now, the healthier and happier you'll be later in life.

Diets full of unhealthy foods cause weight gain and diseases. Too much salt and fat can lead to heart disease. Too much sugar and calories can lead to diabetes. Strokes, bone disease, kidney and liver diseases, and more may all be caused in part by unhealthy diets.

Many people are getting diabetes, mostly because of an unhealthy diet and a lack of exercise. Diabetes involves how the body processes sugar. In a healthy person, a substance called insulin deals with the sugar in your blood. The more sugar you eat, the more sugar is in your blood. Insulin uses the sugar to provide energy for your body. People with diabetes have a problem with how their insulin is regulated. Some people don't produce insulin. They have type 1 diabetes. They have to take insulin and carefully watch what they eat. People with this kind of diabetes are born with it, and it has nothing to do with diet. Many more people have type 2 diabetes. Type 2 diabetes is caused by an unhealthy diet and lack of exercise. In the past, mostly adults got type 2. Today, more and more children and teens are developing it because of a diet filled with unhealthy food and a lack of exercise. A person with type 2 diabetes may have to take medicine, including insulin. Some can manage their disease by eating healthfully and getting exercise. Over time, diabetes usually gets worse. It can lead to problems with the kidneys, eyes, blood flow in feet and legs, and more.

Luckily, eating vegetables now reduces your risk for many of these serious diseases, including diabetes. You can't say with certainty that if you eat vegetables you'll never get sick. But many people are less likely to get sick if they eat plenty of vegetables.

Scientists have studied vegetables and their nutrients. They found evidence that suggests vegetables can reduce the risk of cancer, heart disease, diabetes, and more.

TEXT-DEPENDENT QUESTIONS

1. What does healthy weight mean?
2. How does eating vegetables help you maintain a healthy weight?
3. What is the difference between type 1 and type 2 diabetes?
4. How can eating vegetables help prevent type 2 diabetes?
5. How can eating more vegetables now help you be healthier in the future?

There's no reason not to eat vegetables! The more you eat now, the better off you'll be. Vegetables are an important part of a healthy diet. If you already eat vegetables—eat some more! If you haven't yet discovered that you like veggies, be open to trying them. Try new vegetables you've never tasted. Try them raw or cooked in new ways. Pretty much everyone loves vegetables if they give themselves enough chances to try them.

Once you start eating vegetables, you'll never stop. Include them in every meal, snacks, and even fast-food meals! You'll be healthier today and tomorrow all because you chose to eat those vegetables.

Find Out More

ONLINE

Fresh for Kids
www.freshforkids.com.au/veg_pages/veg.html

Fruits and Veggies More Matters
www.fruitsandveggiesmorematters.org/get-kids-to-eat-fruits-and-vegetables

MyPlate: Vegetables
www.choosemyplate.gov/food-groups/vegetables.html

Staying Healthy
kidshealth.org/kid/stay_healthy

Vegetable Recipes
www.superhealthykids.com/healthy-kids-recipes/category/vegetable-recipes.php

IN BOOKS

Claybourne, Anna. *Healthy Eating: Diet and Nutrition.* Portsmouth, N.H.: Heinemann, 2008.

Graimes, Nicola. *Kids' Fun and Healthy Cookbook.* New York: DK Publishing, 2007.

Kuskowski, Alex. *Cool Eating: Healthy and Fun Ways to Eat Right.* Minneapolis, Minn.: Checkerboard Library, 2012.

Pollan, Michael. *The Omnivore's Dilemma: The Secrets Behind What You Eat, Young Readers Edition.* New York: Dial Books, 2009.

Spilsbury, Louise. *Eat Smart: Vegetables.* Portsmouth, N.H.: Heinemann, 2009.

Series Glossary of Key Terms

Carbohydrates: The types of molecules in food that we get most of our energy from. Foods like sugars and grains are especially high in carbohydrates.

Dairy: Milk or foods that are made from milk.

Diabetes: A disease where the body can't use sugar to produce energy correctly.

Diet: All the foods and nutrients that you normally eat.

Energy: The power stored in food that lets your body move around and carry out other body functions.

Farm: A place where plants and animals are grown and raised to produce food.

Fast food: Food designed to be ready for the customer as fast as possible. Usually it's more expensive and less healthy than fresh food, but it is very convenient.

Fiber: Tough parts of plant foods that your body can't digest. Fiber helps your digestive system function normally.

Fruits: A food group that includes the edible parts of plants that contain the seeds. They are often colorful and have a sweet flavor.

Grains: The seeds of various kinds of grass plant. Grains include rice, wheat, corn, and many others. They are high in carbohydrates and fiber, and can be stored for a long time.

Harvest: The process of gathering crops or the time when crops are gathered.

Local foods: Foods that are grown close to where they are eaten, so they don't have to be transported very far.

Minerals: Materials found naturally in metals or rocks. Our bodies need certain minerals in very small quantities.

Nutrients: Any part of food that our body uses in some way to survive and stay healthy.

Obesity: A state of being so overweight that it's bad for your health.

Organic: A way of producing food in which no genetic modifications, harmful pesticides, or hormones can be used.

Protein: The chemical parts of food that your body uses to build muscles and perform certain body processes. If your body runs out of carbohydrates and fat, it will start using protein for energy.

Vegetables: Plant foods that are usually made of the flower, stem, leaf, or root of a plant. They are usually high in fiber and certain nutrients.

Vitamins: Certain kinds of molecules that your body cannot produce. Instead, you need to get them in your diet to stay healthy.

Index

About the Author & Consultant

Celicia Scott lives in upstate New York. She worked in teaching before starting a second career as a writer.

Dr. Lisa Prock is a developmental behavioral pediatrician at Children's Hospital (Boston) and Harvard Medical School. She attended college at the University of Chicago, medical school at Columbia University, and received a master's degree in public health from the Harvard School of Public Health. Board-certified in general pediatrics and developmental behavioral pediatrics, she currently is Clinical Director of Developmental and Behavioral Pediatrics and Consultant to the Walker School, a residential school serving children in foster care. Dr. Prock has combined her clinical interests in child development and international health with advocacy for children in medical, residential, and educational settings since 1991. She has worked in Cambodia teaching pediatrics and studying tuberculosis epidemiology; and in Eastern Europe visiting children with severe neurodevelopmental challenges in orphanages. She has co-authored numerous original publications and articles for families. She is a also nonprofit board member for organizations and has received numerous local and national awards for her work with children and families.

Picture Credits